The Invention of Culture

Other works by Lisa Samuels include:

LETTERS (Meow Press 1996)
The Seven Voices (O Books 1998)
War Holdings (Pavement Saw Press 2003)
Paradise for Everyone (Shearsman Books 2005)
Increment (a family romance) (Bronze Skull Press 2006)

Lisa Samuels

The Invention of Culture

Shearsman Books
Exeter

First published in in the United Kingdom in 2008 by
Shearsman Books Ltd
58 Velwell Road
Exeter EX4 4LD

www.shearsman.com

ISBN 978-1-905700-85-1

Acknowledgements

Some poems in *The Invention of Culture* have been published by the
following: *Aufgabe*, Bronze Skull Press, *Cant*, *Denver Quarterly*, *Hambone*,
How2, *Intercapillary Space*, *Jacket*, *Oban*, *New American Writing*, */nor*, and
Shadowtrain. Many thanks to all the editors.

Contents

Occident	11
Sunday afternoon	12
Everyone agrees and you have culture	13
Discipline and punish	14
Political poem	16
Civitas	17
Fire skin with the cell-phone execution on	18
Rope theory	25
Choose me	26
Box kite (romantic poetry)	27
Host-nation	28
Lost and found	29
Intimacy parabola	31
Intimacy arc	32
Practice, practice	33
Maze: a play in the round	34
The morning of departure	38
Portrait d'un homme	39
Snakes and eagles never learn	40
Left behind	41
Song: body's end	42
Progress (a lecture)	44
Egyptology	46
Riddle of the covering cherub	47
Constancy to an idealized subject	48
Witness	49
Beneath the valley of the present indicative	51
The five enslavements: a novel in four parts	52
Timber	56
Point of view is expensive	57
The meal of your choice	58
Song: city's end	60
My ex-aesthetics	62

Open your eyes to the terrible sculpture of bedclothes   63
How to turn paper back into a tree   64
The wind howls without the dancers heavily vanish   67
Footage   68
Temporality standing in for freedom from experience   69
Increment (a family romance)   70
I'm not waiting for anything   77
The Body Near as the Sea (a poem dance)   78
Young and beautiful   79
Apraxia   80
Social sculpture   81
Anacoluthon   83

for Mark and Rowan

That we are permanent temporarily, it is warm to know, though we know no more.

Emily Dickinson

OCCIDENT

I took a walk and fell into blindness as
  the grass bright hitting
I walked and was forsaken by avenues

     (underneath location was 'a chance to guess'

Walking I was surrounded by hysteria the forms
of dogs and flowers in archetypal
  would-be heat, women across their wishes

I fell to an imagined countenance
assuaging their comportment
the garden gestures partial with bells
and heavy tresses
  I will without omniscience having
never meant to mean the bells are flying
east to west, into straight lines pitch and drill

     hollow out your back with greengrass, hallowtree
      forsaking hysterical luxury made plain)

  by walking's bellows
delicate around your arms ideas of dogs
drawn see-through so the walk's achieved
as pennants for those dogs, bright fluttering

SUNDAY AFTERNOON

Maybe permanence is something you're born with
a soft arbitration of children with their open mouths
the sun slant at the parlor and women milling forcefully
arrange each licit article upon the tongue
in profile, as to say lemon
arbitrary
sweet
against the nostril
a little tang of wishing in the strawberry

Just like when you strayed too far
from your 'felt sense of purpose'
some names attached to the story to give it flesh
a passel of ideas shaped like persons: they were
wattled, habitual in covert languages
held together shimmying like property
two fine bones, two fine hands
the little wrenches in between
inscrutable barometers in a weather

Perplexed inflexibility as 'not her fault at all'
and anyway like the bird who rushed down the chimney
covered with its death
parting the hair like trees

EVERYONE AGREES AND YOU HAVE CULTURE

The elect, morphemically engrossed
is beautiful, his haunch par terre
like the horsey appended to a carousel
whose figures of motion self-deceive.

'Safari,' he's telling me about it, one exquisite
fortitude after another. We purr on land
in grasses, on highways made of carpet
the pinks of funerary curiosity

Not that economy isn't the central basis of
blood terror, but the woman in the cake
knew how to get out of there fast
(he did it, he stayed right there in his doubt!)

They all smiled enormously their boundaries
lightened. After that, one might hope to *be thinking*.
Hyperions of crème brûlée, cities
one would heretofore have no reason to spell.

DISCIPLINE AND PUNISH

the logic of my nature
is triumvirate
circumscribed by anxious latitudes

not alone in this
unburied longing
   perhaps the fee can be arranged

      flecked underneath
       like jade pilings
      planted in water, infiltrate

the fruits of my orchard are wanting
the clasp of impairment
rendered silent

heaving through clarity
like a ladylike sigh
inveterate fortune
   falls triumphant

         I have struck oil
         I have struck land
         I have struck your face
         with the back of my hand

         anything you see that I want
         anyone you know that I have
         fortunate and unvariable
         chalked on the listening board

the building rumbles
in the floor of my chest
　you, knowing something
halt by the wall

descending to a non-escape
the fire begins at the top of the air
　　and sweeps incredibly down

Political poem

the vocabulary one could say in subst
        ituting itself as moronically sashes
a body's rhythms give it density

        painting always had its idea
        a pose in the process of dissolving but
the flicker book merely replete
      says the luminous   in calling such

        things inimical to beacon
the standard three-by-four happens
on an edge

        having created a single autonomy
        between passable images of magic
    forth over and over two locations
        inside one inter
          locutor compositing no longer as
         theatrical backdrop but
phantom lapse, accommodation fantasies.

   we observe they occupy
   two places at once and I
     never did see or fetch a re   prehensive finally

what I mean is detached
kindly, floating in
mention, no particular
space in mind

CIVITAS

No, don't get that – back from it, we are
too apparent each, all commas and elucting
what nature gave us, 'ick' – forestall whatever
it is you: and never mind the 'we are climbing out'
when you abide or that!, inscrutable timetable
up dearly, how it plains us for a game: one go
and you are always monument, a saken
optimist flying saturate via some
air or error-striven behemoth
hitting the cloud-belt with a prrup!,
so that we're shook and unbesaddled
with a bell or supine entity that makes
us addle-stocked and mildly whipped –

Fire skin with the cell-phone execution on

You whose rates are finer than dynamite you whose rants
are closer than my heart you who dropped 5,000 tons
of destructive material from your head and you

I cannot reach – I cannot try up pry – I fearly, wanton calibration
of no earth, no riot-chore strung round your arms
no lights up stock-tick lyric-blaster you

soft and weakened state, the lines around your balance show
I have you now, your soft negated strafe worn on

the earth is calm, it folds and wriggles it has given me the yes
and I am holding it withal, the yes and I havoc the strands

yes I habiting, the whole relentless particle you said
the wind has saned for who the strands done softly she

so awful touching under smiles earth has given
navigant to fine pushed-out whole calendar sweat

and shoed the bidding struck with numerable arms
soft tense hold biotic brace and you me so so words with touch

and are so let to be the hands you gently
world in habits own and this the uppermost

the pensive fair that blanch gone linger,
monger hands see say they listen hear

that they cannot want for power
that they cannot reap and proffer to you power that
they are tense and mobile in
        your arms back sense of time
            sheets winding around your eyes

the arms have you the rope has you
over your head your neck and soft
wrinkled against the obfuscate surroundings and
what comes next and they are calling the sounds
accumulate and you are not sure exactly when

You can cut your heart and instruments
you can put up all the resistance you want
but finally it comes to the broken habits of culture
stringing up your bad-ass hard-won fate

the eyes are torn out the eyes
the knees are giving way the knees
the soft water of the womb is giving way
the home is crushed the eyes can't
see in front of them they are too bad and anguish
     anguish cannot stand the requirements cannot
      stand the broken habits they cannot calibrate
                      what is
    coming over you
             attenuate pretend I'm broken-eyed
    to find my broken-sided
  hard-gone know
           exhausted word, useful to me nothing
    that is fair
        the world is the flattened obscenitor
   of its own berated core
  and backward flap the libertines
    make hard this ifness
          flat out as it rocks

It is the house with panels
the lovely blue puckered out behind
you the birds in the stupid glass
round eyes of the dead
book licking the center of your hand
in her soft imagined sweater

'What name?', did you erase as well –
    (the dark scene with an instrument
    mouth open and ready to collapse)

The news has come by honestly
        and tired I want broken-back voices to your eyes
        'I want a muse sense on my skin, man,'
        approaching they have breached wait
with hands tied round your head
so soft with arms against anticipate

the whole tender scene is one we're saving to the hard drive
        you know, the obsolescent lily child-set
        you kept yourself to take out cold
        the particle-board you bought the bus
            for gleaming non-instructed anyway you want
                the backward slash parts
                    on the rope your soft cloth throat
                    between so you don't know

they are snareware holding you
they are hard-tipped barnacles
in your drowning comprehension
the quartermost option of your skin
tired eyes tried heat
baked arms fold forward
implements, flat evidential
stream obtuse – most willingly

so tired of breach,
of arteries pitch scream brought back
cloud absence in my ears

They smile disingenuous the man –
I have held your arms with my head
made you not-mine with a vengeance

      you are a stream
      particle a dugout
      dirt bank strewn
      recollect you are
      lulling your head impassable
      lavish dread has me in no
      tentacles out ink in every mine

      Resist the minutes near you better harangue
      drop easy you hold lament, the perch oasis
      rendering you finical, molecular
      of each other no discretion plucked the act

          please don't knock on my door
            she is arms gone legible tiny things
              to tie my mouth around

Rope theory

Knowledge reverts to type
lacking a subtext. experience. a girl with ringlets
in her eyes, testing the long pages
with boyish mien. unimpeachable, like gardens.

Outdoors, we can't see anything.
a disilluminate set of trees
fronts only itself, dowager forest
lavishing the upturned faces of birds.
calmly we have a name for this
version of events. your billow answers to it.

Theocracy's a name for costly garments
made occasion for a never-do upend.
they separate willingly, recall the gardens
in irregular rows, come up for any price
but your perfection. neither youth nor age
especially, no temperance for resistance to be.

Underneath experience is experience. no
part of realization glows willingly
to pasture items. some perspective, good
for you. the soft sides undevoured
for fingers, the habits activate for calm
flow willingly, compiling reasonable
suppressions in the skin. known
for its folding attributes of wait.

CHOOSE ME

there were some barriers – stood up with accordions
and played for my head – I heard the middle
where someone enveloping a self – the door is wide
and women flow through it – they are 'like'

stone lined out as we ascend – people shaped
assumingly – 'the air is thin and even young girls gasp'
like a body filling sky with – perceptual inclinations

later, men with drums sang – no deliverance
more flat-top hooligans I wager – having paid that debt
my back lacerate with grasses – floating betimes in sullen 'sea'
a lake mistake – and there you are, triumphal

holding me at bay – again a saying it, a gentle stupor
in your breath I feel the intake – of obedience
telling yourself – repeat 'choose me choose me'

Box kite (romantic poetry)

It is a bird, it was a bird, it flew over

somewhere the rim has found itself

funneling through grasslands, and is divested

of obsequious longings, the wished-for corners

gliding away though not in cramps,

not ever moribund.

Unhurt, she felt the sides again

soft-polished to a landed sympathy

that takes you outside, 'perhaps

you could tell me what it tastes like.'

A gentle monstering has presence

instead of the languid ashy form I saw

here raisable figurines pushed up

to be sunken, inevitable edges

like the tree you think you see

particulars from a distance

HOST-NATION

prolate spheroid becomes me, true
the other side of just in case
I own the limpid metal
of your feet, my dear, that faraway
head a cake of nails

get used to topicality
sleek and sleepy sun aloop
above his breast the wind
the present lofts like plastic
sheaths the scene

prophetic body parts are sad
for those who can't divide
their times, the kneecaps wandering
from their narrowness
to a broad uncategorical ideal

LOST AND FOUND

The sky is grey and actual, the rain high and actual
    has you met – a mad pin in your heart
  in your shoulders the broken Halifax your head on the stone
    of nothing more than ok

you are 'paraseduced' at last – your own smile at the plans
  all round your body fixed, his broken voice
immensely re-bargained with broken eyes no more akin to task
    not waiting with egregious suggestion
      nor any 'putative' alliance
        to show you promise for

                – the islands are screaming forbear
                  voices are completely histrionic
                      and vocality?
           the trees habituate and cars strewn
              futurely beside a futureless
                enormity with a laid lack
            of your own

  bridgeway – let's give it out that she is streamless, a face
peeled back to see the recurrent prolixity of fact –
    the holding of your arms by one who says
      'did you did you' and why
        you know desire will be very upset
      on the beach, the actualized events

  in broken paper we are simply staring down the argument
    for its own sake, as ornamental as it is
      saturate with perturbed realizations
  of dependence, a brief hiatus – promised strings clipped some
        and taken to his hideaway Broken Hat

broken voice harumphing til the pain is legible, is enormously
        curtained

                      – the islands are screaming they have fish
                      nibbling at their innards and birds
                      who sing and *will not stop*
                      they have footsteps cracking and
                      women starting angrily they have
                      self standing
                      insolently wishing

to respire – it could ever finish she said oh yes that expresses
        on the nails hand holding to stop from saying
whisked, the favored opportunity was over before we recognized
        this thing no not that you do not
                you are a promise, a saturation

  circumstance, the islands whimper softly in their greed,
      they need any voices please
          how dirt speaks of admonishment
    and tired not more plentifully
      themselves so blessed with the actual

INTIMACY PARABOLA

as in: you shrinking to receive: agape
or 'forness' given to procure ends: these we wit
and witting have them: you notched over with
me to be half-sure: not for nothing have we
met and in the skinned half-time do we
take: high deep and in the pressure of not telling
the tower beset and garnered: you are shirted
still not bestable: not for something do you
keep yourself at bay: on either end of experiment
the navy juncture sits fondling itself convinced
that it has up!, and not a notch too soon or
we will down!, and not a crippled architect
to find us: being green and all to make
us mighty in our common: the ground is flesh
the flesh is air the air is paper the buildings
are arches of idea and we:

Intimacy Arc

the high seas want to be near us
they are loverly
the air wishes to be inside itself
it is onerous
water is what we put upon
our lips and it
is what we tell each other when
we speak with water
earth is dirt and gets inside
is honorific
take your fingers and give them
back themselves
to make the ambuscade of blood
an unforseeing
adjure could bring itself to suture
each hand to hand
until you walk there with your beaches
very still and

PRACTICE, PRACTICE

Victim of the sentimentalizing of jeux d'esprit, she was like a
movie shot tight against the waist. Practice, practice. Hold my
pink hand as we put it through the shade – in Louisiana,
in Mexico. Playhooks holding up the bones.

To which we must add, curious and experience, your convivial
clothes drop instantly to the floor. What is an innocent conductor
doing with effluvia? Naïveté, distinctly not a room, white flakes
falling over lawns. Haven't I heard this

Now ethics. We've been I guess charging prudence her brief life
domed. No enlargement across the bow, though we 'come about'
shock pioneers at sail. Much as I told you, your eyes having lunch
in the little town of my face.

Your practice has arrived at the door, illumination prior to its
opening. In any case, we can always get up. Earth's presumptuous
sublimity we're looking for. Between the precise distinctions
memory is congenital, the nipple circles closed.

MAZE: A PLAY IN THE ROUND

(Act I)

Alightened

in arriviste trances

these moving theme projectiles

thistle wind shoots past the barbaric

posterior arrangements, enhanced difficulties

   it isn't fondling that deranges
    your weather shoot, your brave departures

In order to commence the great kindle-lesson
we might undo its heathen fortitude:
you know, the one we folded
over the feverish and insomniac
theatrical tea-girl

she waited all afternoon and couldn't serve

Just when the part beveled into two, the place marked
'here' went semi-comatose

    which meant
       its eyes were permeated with longing

Though in the forfeitures we measure
uncountable opportunities for crashing, for heaping
for dialectical clover-leafs where

    we drove the new automaton
    she wants to look
    the window through but cannot, her eyes are sealed
    with pre-descent cement, you peeled and peeled
  and only got created

The sack with the cradle-thought
meets it dual flower mimic
and 'there' is the route where shots exchange

(*Act II*)

    doesn't your contrition suit
    the bandage clothes you constantly

    when I gathered up the curtains
    they were swaying, they articulated

Your humor is inoperable, it gashes
through the clearing of your held-back
heat, and nothing but ice-knives
might approximate

when you thought
thought crumbled
as the undergrowth

I cannot make the engine be anything other than
what

(*Act III*)

Your topical departing
went ghostly

   honorific
         kinetics, peripatetic clones

   it isn't as though
    is forms
   airs like that

The cloak finds its figure
the pick finds its star
in eyes, in eyes

      fleeing from the autographic
      your lithesome dimensionhood

Two garish figurines are better than none
but none rules, she has a claim

on the inner skin of my upper body
I see the attentive marks
blue and purple and white and red
mummish fallings

(*Act IV*)

Protect me from tenacity

if in the haunted ink there is
a ferocity model
let him be an effect

The finest interwoven cloth could hold her mouth
bound and indefinite

in the aspirant strands shooting from your eyes

Causeness leads to distance
operational assumptions overcome
'there is nothing to be wished for'

all the polished antitheticals
are pent and spilled and rued

on the path of eyeishness, the lines intrude

THE MORNING OF DEPARTURE

Don't mean that – mean that

it is going to Rain

Do you see? I see

no, I don't see

I hear – what do you

say to me now?

Ahora?

Dichten, condensare, the vertigo girl

erased in her own

condemnitude – no quieren decir que

decir que, arriving

to be opposite

va a llover – is it like that

at last?

PORTRAIT D'UN HOMME

The judge and the boy went together to the snowbank. The future
was waiting in the form of imagination. Brackets and immolation
came next to the sea. He meant everything at once, even when
the ice set up in pockets. Reaching in, the boy burned his digits
again and again. The judge took him by the hand and led him
through the snows. It was an unreal city, the banks bowed deeply
to the north in spite of disestablishment. Houses, houses, houses.
The sea rose with ideas. Each one of his hairs was gently tugged
in multiple directions, while he smiled. Better than arrows.
The gentle spirit recited to him in modulated tangerines. He always
recalled. Each dove fluttered its way on to his shelves, announcing
all the flowers, tigers, elves. They were gentle too.
The judge was friendly with everyone on the bench.

SNAKES AND EAGLES NEVER LEARN

The dawn is tightly folded
Sapphic lisp, demotic splat
the high prediction of your footsteps
tropicality, green audience paid
before the missile hits
a dying response induced by soft nutrition

Mutual problem fields come to mind – which
Caravaggio in the first place?
the behaviors we call art primarily take
the narrative corpse of technically
millennia, as though the particular were
small creatures in extreme informational chaos

Your posh obstreperous arms are
protosocial homebase circling
and the little animal wakes up without haste
– a yawn of providential help –
then slips and poses as cartoon
het up for salutary speech

A Sapphic grin gone wastrel grim
more ink boys flexed for multiparts
in derivation sets, we hear
– the lucent animal flushed
postlit on adaptation's groove –
the dyad pays you though
not to be true

LEFT BEHIND

Go to the opening – look – she was wanting what the rose meant
or hesitating at the boundary, women wishing with their heads
a fire, a replacement article reaching out

the girl gave herself a name – in the city she was a happening
linked to fervent wish, accompanied to call it – incontinuity
unable to fend herself the absolute

conveyance keeps us tripod, standing for reasons
not ours, the sun lifting up air that doesn't wish it
dark settling over things that don't
a lonesome given to sense, after all

you were a bright set of keys, a forked violence
severally lined up in taut bonanzas, and here
with the hullabaloo the torture is pacific
a register of its going-to-have-occurred

SONG: BODY'S END

Even with your headlessness a model of infinity brushed away

    the outside airs are miracle replacements
    invested with the animation of false beds

a step on the stair, a door effortless with misspent departure

The last thing left in the box I wear with constancy
removed into pallors of looking for
      resistance to air
                 Although you might imagine

convictions of other hands and eyes, how
they fumigate desire into flight   There will be
     feasts, expected ruptures of the ideal picture

       after the reading of the readable scene
         there will be readings alongside those
       that rip up emulation even here

The purpose looks like home, a slaking of the dirty thirst
  and eyes that make illuminating glue

    arrest the churches through the billowing
      of serviced air   whose open ceilings
            aim toward your hands

    imagine carving circles in that air, no paths
to be accused of   like creation
               The beauty

is that no one notices, legs and arms have all
the fun, wet lungs convert what hangs delight

above the lifting eyes   disornament is
a regular tearing up of the dirt of meaning

Progress (a lecture)

There is a mechanism for beauty, I think – kind eyes
blurry eyes, fortuitous sight mode fret.
To hanker, that was it. A grievance felt through stones
to trees. In that city language fierce defined.

Otherwise, telling us we'd always wanted to hear
the man accords soft-bellied clouds
disclosing gently for the erudite. Now we can go in

> *such dissolutions green or red*
> *or shot through vinyl crackling*
> *designations filled with smoke*
> (The young frame forces us to hop,
> the lean vampire gives me the screens.)

Thank you for coming along. Almost forty years ago
a constant stream. And holding hands
thinking for the event
dividing into half-lights
                          dozens. As a poet admirable
                seas that stead in bark or find
        repressed maintains.
                We are novel in a scene hold, late last year.

Viewing platform, whence
the monitor rose and trembled
air's motility. Marked by public intellectuals
curating the windows with relentless idea.
'I make my life in England and France'
grateful for the marks and accolades
                (This material is pretty raw, after all
                fairly processed tongue or book. It fields

in some quite general terms. Most
especially
      at this place in 'France', the house lights
      good as they come and convivial.)
Lights against the body, small tenacious

Prefix asides, this prudential town owes the
ministerial
as the words ripple with what 'draw' could
  redisburse. Lion's legacy is
     shrink to Francophone. The man's skin
    while the village burns its regional centre of culture.
Artistic actions (emphasize those words).

Thirty years of British sculpture drops to the floor.
The value it seeks to return is worth noting.

EGYPTOLOGY

Can you be tipped up, like bear toes
on sullen grass? Or invent obedience
like molecules given to industrial fire?
I say you have as much chance as a pyramid
scaling its own backside with a crazed disobedience
as if.
      Now that cloture is a sure thing, we
can stop communicating after all. Your own
besotted atmosphere is 'willy-nilly-silly'
like his little aspirations huge beside the
coming-to-be-near-you-ness that I once had.
Nor are we periwinkle nor miscreant or ever were.
      He's made of poppycock notions
while in the cornice underneath your pillow
is a hard fact nowhere near kin to facticity,
as I keep telling them: or if we focus or if we don't
upon the spin will we discover or obtrude
a ready point?
      If you think about it, rain
wouldn't fall the same on pyramids anyway,
the camels and fixed notions being what they are.

RIDDLE OF THE COVERING CHERUB

Grim as an obtuse parameter, I have no limbs

a dubious secondary wakefulness, my eye open
in fetching avocation rolling awkward

toward you or picked up as though a watchful
pose could find me dangling the foster-driven

mandates of this dream, long-hoped-for

subcutaneous miracles, what earth
to your availing hands will waken me

to prove an admonition, the orchard of
something natural that artifice becomes

little smiles lest my rueful contents fail
in the air of my suture-self, fond voice

capped in a vortex, not so toggled
gracefully up and down the sky

follows when I'm let out

CONSTANCY TO AN IDEALIZED SUBJECT

the freeway spinning delicate behind
a non-committed pair of lips
to you it seemed incomparable, natty,
an omnipresent earthquake
I hear languishing in the bed device
also moving, as though tears

the truck, you said, was on its wheels
and ammunition glaring, stop right there
to canvass eyes, the sullen mouth around
speaking has no pretensions
wields no sooner aid than
we spoke

'on the radio, I hear sounds of
shouting,' so they are not here
though something performs the graded road
grows like waiting with scarified longings
another to lullaby completely
among fiction stations, alongside
this flower and that rapacious
nesting creeper, one that shows
it's nice to have the elements cooperate

as the wide moat reaches
symmetry, what we speak of compensates
and you surrounded pray for
double-sided baskets to help find us
swimming in the tender acid
of our mouths

WITNESS

In finite mathematics of sway

minded axes hew their way

his fingered linings rent

sailing in the frozen air, not by degrees
but miming the pedestrian

The weakening signals collapsed for him, though he
shaped his hands accomplishedly throughout

*

Having heard quick meaning amperes

as cured as ivory creaking through the face

your horns discover freaked alternatives

and then you tuck tuck tuck

I found the aspish hospices of speech
abiding carelessly under a gather

what squirming cover meant to each irregular

driven through the tongue

*

never enough attitude to keep
left-overs of your consequential scrapings, non-me
lining thinner of non-you

what two talks put together
a clinical dispersal

Stop and build
metastasis, the burgeoning impulses to breathe
shaped errors

standing there, among the creamy anguish of physical

while head-top, green-top, neck-stopped apertures
look at you

BENEATH THE VALLEY OF THE PRESENT INDICATIVE

She spoke with an assurance
that hourclocks were invisible that they rode through air
on putty wagons and were rare like spinning
suits inside a mouth

Tight gunny sacks
forced in and said arrange the plates
round and unavailable like sound sheets in the air above
salt flats or sky

Otherwise
the buried animals made themselves
ill for better keeping as though labels found
a promised land

that never goes away,
the sentence doled out narrow
in the slot behind your head while round about
it slips the world

THE FIVE ENSLAVEMENTS: A NOVEL IN FOUR PARTS

Chapter 1: We hold ourselves eventful

In those clouds figures ignite, shadows are visitable outlines
at the back of rooms – I have a club and pointer holding them
upright, or I am ill-dressed and need to be given a blue shirt,
a red shirt, something deep offsetting the plain strangeness
no one 'has' (but betting it) any plans nor I fixate on a trompe-
l'oeil can tell you

a dog barks in the patio, he is stuck forever in a moving
position – seeming delicate wings on the sky tip-top, the lit
approaches gather up their meanings to take them home
or canvas tells itself without dementia, though I stand looking
like a crazy without wheels

All the patio given to itself without reprieve, the nice ones
smiling you know it's really sincere, the caustic ones wheeling
and twirling intention on their fingers: from the corners where
the dancers have no experience, you will be swallowed up
in dark ideas of art

She of the falling down has a box of half-done paints, a man
called Ah-very gives you – he is old and safer that way, though
longing fetches through his latches

Sorrow, it is sorrow to get somewhere you don't efface nor half-
belong – to soft-formed people moving in their shadows,
they know 'how to be' there, company procured

Chapter 2: In medias res

Finished with nothing, distended on the float balloon
we'll ball the floor in wax to make it 'ours,' little tree,
little somnolent fixing the posh names, bobble-headed
experimenters toggling back their throats to song ravishing
the air with a what-you-will of having lived, setting up
their own distended consequence – it isn't 'fair' that it
should be obvious, evidence brought in to make the social
scene dismayed

here is a red house, here a blue the white manifest, staves
in the arms hold down, the legs apparent stimuli for walking,
me on a sidewalk boat, floating whereness to its gradual
display: 'come see!' that the evidence is impressive you
will surely grant, and me and something obvious and green

Chapter 3: Orthodox squinting

Or clay or ice or snow – mixt it is forestalled for an honest
plan adventure, the girly figures racing through the streets
in ties, in moxy scrambling, duked and inadmissable

to the play!, where we will randomly admit ourselves
reversed, the silly people wholly to the side without
coincidence they can sludge on us, we'll find curtains
lace and symbols to drape over the statues of consequence
leering on the scene – the flesh-eating ideas make us
dizzy, underlying first principles with messy admonitions:
do! this thing or do not awaken, that is a mistake I tell you
to forestall your disappointment

Chapter 4: Blur

You've made a place for scrupulous delay, the fulsome bite
of syllables, mouthy extras, the 'what we do not need' printed
pack-wise on your parts

People gathering to look are soft walls made to mirror anyone
listening as the loudspeaker conjures its display, a scene of
variable postures, the sound of protest wafting sideways over
an air we haven't traced so carefully this time – disembodied
voice-making, little throats leaning backward to make a pointed
distribution of something *valuable* or 'valid,' a plain tinkering
we've done with dismay – from far away a will subscribed to our
importunate venturing; they *must* or 'we will ... we will ... we
will ...'

having said with forcefulness the voice looks wet-eyed to
its fortress: don't tell anyone, a coeval exchange with particles
we've got hammered in our throats cancer-like, lid-like, some
forest symbols all round our minds – the time is tipsy-top,
hivsies havesies about it really, location being what it is and
your resistance down, the frowns inside your lashes finally fixed
or 'finally' enduring their own temperance

You see with a fine-boned distribution over other girls who
listen to – the ship overboard, a promise to someone who isn't
even here as though disparagement were 'to answer to' the clouds
whether or no you have obeyed – while laundry-like cycles spin
just past the birds gathering to announce outside the city, a lone
dolly parading up and down with all the answers inapplicable
to questions that you know

TIMBER

The beauty of self-arrested purity sits across from me

on the train. a few more nobs of oxygen proving history.

Our Lady of the Dollars isn't his finest work, no matter:

without a nation-state, you're free to superimpose.

Social doughnuts, pansy skies, the burlesque nausea

of the city. The presentation of calamity as the surest sign

of mimetic reasonableness. *The soft manicure of reference*

closets its indices. He must have painted the heads on last.

POINT OF VIEW IS EXPENSIVE

says the man, who lifts it to his ears
and jiggles, as if to pattern acquiescence to a meaning

not so much reaching as imbibing, it's explained
to me, as we walk through boys to reach

desire, a map that toys with corners
for attributes of binging girl ice cream

she's striving to be seen – 'wait for me' – I'm following
the orders given by so many, the shrift deliverance

'come here and let me waste your chance' so
amenable and far away it hardly matters

to a sequence we've forgotten to measure with
the boys – who having announced their willingness to parrot

repeat their names to anyone, 'will move in synchrony
to please in hopes,' their thinful bodies placing

in the lights what grievance sings – then
you shepherd, you announce, and we keep getting to

transpiration, the boxes on the wall as if explaining
translucence in the head, sick willful

given to noise, to repetition's dalliance, to dreams of boys
who point toward a venture undertaken, publicly announced
but never three-dimensional or here

THE MEAL OF YOUR CHOICE

Yesterday alongside tractor wishes
and ransomed fleshly arts
    you spoke: opalescent, magistrate leanings

        as though involuntary
        as though eyes

with longing listening, whistled parthenogenesis
        I lost them
                streaming in the lake

      a partial benediction, ice cream tabled
      the cool bowl under my pillow

that was a small closed building
you found yourself

        smudgy curtains

        systematic exegesis

        white eyes falling globally

Sold to be in pieces, I tripped that 'please'
    aright the sand hour

  it approaches, with a solitary   hunger story, would you give dry mountains, all these bones wrought

I wean you, necromantic soldiery
whistling

    – do you coo here, do you nautical serene? –

I found your trapping coterie
  fields, rowing

        forward in a claustrophobic sea

     you reached roundabout
           that dark

      angled, and the new one
      rising board by board

feather talk arranged, admonishing
 the back which holds you

to a rare and bracketed smile
        woven outward, that's a waiting

  taking all the fire
     breathing in

      – do you hold that piecing next to you? –
      why the whisper, folded peroration?

SONG: CITY'S END

A catching pause is where we meet to keep
caused charges in the rain, bare limbs outside
   increasing coverlets
    (it's lavish in the lovely green jacket, how it holds)

One time in fun it ran, sleeves flapping and
   judicious resurrection of internals felt
   and feeling made the random stick

    beat away that perfect gap between
    how-it-not and has-it-gone, suffusion
knowing all the artifice of stopping and

    Futurity as the better of the rest, one friend observing
in the papered air he knows what holiness
you strive for meets, not having had to find
not having far, by half observantly

    it will be always clearer in to passage on
     this way, always than the planning
       first aimless then
    the random building then the fullest form that shows
      itself embodiment refuses.

Can it resurrect, enough to make the world
clear stripped of varnish blink incessantly?

Or is such interposing just a marvel that the human makes
   you telling me 'words might seek truth
   instead of themselves,' fuller between

the streams of _____ and _____. It must be
    continually impassible the ones I seek

and buck against with surest fire of hands
and eyes, as though to burn were achievement
  more than rescue

My ex-aesthetics

here is the wall meant for leaning, the place

built against the door, the

        apparition shadowing

   the

          translucent imagery

the finest pieces imaginable

     I want

        taking endlessly

the whole system

    rots our bellies to this kind of sin

beleaguered, alluded, simplified

all the artistry of evasion can do

OPEN YOUR EYES TO THE TERRIBLE SCULPTURE OF BEDCLOTHES

1
Kenneth Koch held three oranges, waiting for the bus.
The oranges were self-mesmerized: each was one side of his
four-sided-self. He was taking the bus to present his ideas.
He had to keep his sole awake (fourth side) awake.

2
'I had to be somewhere.' Meanwhile (unconscious in the cold
house. the only way for it was strategic neglect. out of the array
of definitions) A book of oranges. Where was Kenneth Koch,
and who now alive holds him tenderly?

3
The harbour, that extended palliative, moated gently against
the definition of sea. Animals and the surface was all there.
The air, too, shot with waves mis-heard their dry unfetterings.

4
I understand all the time the room on the other here. procured
again. In certain parts of earth a heart beats – the landscape
he sees is not. he loves registered.

HOW TO TURN PAPER BACK INTO A TREE

1

The pliant boards are tumbling this house, where we are
   subtle as airy fish
            absent the sea   compliant coloring
                    and your bright face

    'Like this,' your virtues tending to abate
   a day-struck wind – the earth beneath
    'hath trembled individually'
                      to wheel us off

   your skin drawn out and pulsing slight
  head up, arms and breath surmounting
              high above the city, palm fronds
        staging   sway

     The hands untempered now one knows
parenthesized slow time
         in difference from story there, the arms grown tired
          as though to mention names

   the task is bare, the lips are warm   the air has balmed
       and made us well reversed

2

    you move – a hazard met
   with lovely want, the hilly trope steering us
            as though we never lived   nor knew
      the coins dropped in our ears

'we know what's what,' the task-born
folding wisdom in the tent   hands reach
fitful semblance, knowing echo is the motor
its telling   paints my tongue, flesh moving – 'I will' –

determined to open or close the earth
ruth cupped   on skies of sound

we'll be in backward wood
by water wishing boys of skin

to rope the rupture inside-out   they tell us
their convictions: 'hey, surrender me'

pick up the fence and wear it in a mesh
around your soft convicted
thighs, all dense with sight the words
are miracles of spite, completely meaning what
they completely say

as a child impermanently tells you   'this is what I want'
the beckoned furniture of day
                                             stones
piled in air, birds as trees

3

your eyes inside the water see
absolution's harmony, that is
partial, it indicts
        itself completely pleased

and we at once in cradle light
　　with books inside our fingertips
　　　　to learn what need to make, to want
　　　　　　the wide paths stonier by day
when you arrive with 'paid for' – luck's
　　　　a final breath particular, of course
　　　　the dog stays in the written world

THE WIND HOWLS WITHOUT THE DANCERS HEAVILY VANISH

The aisle is full of noisy disregard
lavish visual magnificence primarily acoustic
were they followed? (*I'm blind, I'm blind, please hear me!*)
Very suggests. Promise your symbolic evacuation, master,
the release of the burden of objects.

The floor knocks under common bundle
conspicuously unremarked. A triple sense
whose deep notes match as if
the contrivances of variation were wandering return.

A fearful sound late in the scene
thump thump
an inner storm unlike dialectical
roar

I think I see an anti-mind limiting its effects.
a funeral bell and the polis rest assured.
contrariwise, fallen nature traffics in a benison.

Interpret your wooden slavery from another perspective
deeper than the plummet sounds
raucous hap, this island alone
arranged out of confusion
lying somewhere between

FOOTAGE

A hologram has landed. It's divested, tourniquet leaning. Not that
the city could change our walking through it clicka clack, orange
buildings pressing on the water. Form ranted in my brain, like.

Emissary. On the train, ship, car, foot, bus, on the restaurant.
The noons. In the funnel, your holographic spectacle. Inside
the elevator, stairwell, front seat, marble, chill.

The window eyes a soft dilution, robin redbreast book uncovered.
The cabinet bills an overture: peeling sweater, smiling tree. Spring
loads a lolly past the dense event: more rivers convince themselves
the children rest there, tall sycamore for

the rock sits grand. Legs on it. Ships sail fast and few. Girls boys
crowd, tall buildings rest their futures against her softened shoulder.
We will delve wires through it make it stand secrete the paper
lodges inside wares we'll aim for when the moment each how could.

TEMPORALITY STANDING IN FOR FREEDOM FROM EXPERIENCE

Were your manifest assumptions delicious
trigger points, the executable sign
paper torn a little at one edge to make it fleshy

though calmly in my arms the buildings lie
bested into happiness, lie breathing
layers of masculine demise

not necessarily the 'literal,' you conceive
the glorious substitution of a mouth
scurrying back and forth from have to lack

in the dull obsequy of that request
she covered her eyes with silver disks
        smiling half-presently

INCREMENT (A FAMILY ROMANCE)

Sing ruse of famish contumely
they act out of aggression & display
of clatterly feeling, they of
whether or no, sing, historically
the infant holds old women in his arms
they pray, sway, rueful admonitions rise
like churches, a village of churches
a house there smack amidst –

of willy nilly harvest, small ablutions
little plants – sing of that, morses
of clavicles, the shoulders dancing upward
as though ringing hollow musculatures
of sing – men growing backward, portions
given to their ways of arriving, of
skirts, pins, prejudice, the old bright
woman's brighted eyes apeak as when

the trees no long green keen of
their wake, dementia particles, potatoes
soft as evergreens in piles historical
each bare rod of arm extends directions
flattened throat, boys on the map
they drive, every leg in shorts, bare
ruse of costuming

———————————

A sticking joint that closes, air & temperance
having moved the baby, nonce
and habitude resulting landing
in a random place

———————————

Of naught, in that place, was her
backward man broaching subject
hood, the patient waiting having
subsidized her song, we weld
the parchment into pavement modes
that hold blue graduals, with a stitch
of locust purposeful embed

———————————

Air shark, sing, tell of when magnanimity
outswore her place, old woman pale in harbor,
concrete fixtures for a wish in that direction –

She was south, she west, then again bimural
knew after all the potency of rivers

to wash out the skin, prepare it for
our stoniness, the insides of her palms
given to mode, pebbles that will locate

Outside relation – of this accord
rely, involution's special someone
stood for pillage, as if countryesque
he sucked the grasses, stood awhile
and full provided rupture with a straw

———————————

The stitches fell out slowly – of the festival
of falling they were ware, tripped out,
a temperature of celebrated newness
which accompanied that further piedmont
the tree afloat amidst a fest, of that
the woman growing backward could
relate – a far-fetched mandense
hunting venture, one of water, of a man
standing with designs atop his skull –
a direction of full syllables, all establishing
a modal operance of transmutation, betterment,
some indefatigable wishing, prayer-like

Her arms were a vehicular possession
as she lay cross-legged on the grocery floor –

the child forward creasing her ideas with
moat-indifference, soft family layers
bubbling to and fro

———————————

'I remember,' she ensconced, 'future measures
that endeared us' and woke knowing

———————————

The skin was the transition – in it
we could lace apartheid, rite of asking
the child directions, hobble one upon the other
in a milquetoast range that passes
bone to bone – each one a rousing
indefinite that kisses the next end,
'telos hobbles crunchy in the hasp'

———————————

Brother sighs 'and call me when I see'
sister, playing in the surf of the river
he looks barring, funded by recreation
for its sovereign incapacity to allay.

She waits to tell the outlines, stones,
with chisels in her teeth she clumps
and wears. White boxes are the kind
conceit of lining up to coexist, as if
somehow that's o.k., promises accepted,
notes crusted in a code on keys inlaid
in the bars of a piano. Tuned.

The mother is invested, her hands
inverted colors on the bedspread hoard,
ignoble surfacing. She knows the flesh
as incandescent, operatic strafing turning
all the sheets to mush – that too as caring
crazy at the wheel, ambulatory nonsense
flashing her periodic breakdowns – come
and get it!, calls the child in her ambitions,
no more dogged than seemly, the ink
dripping in her veins . . .

———————————

Brother waits concretely, asphalted above
its claims, each shape a reminder of
something not entirely forgot – as in a

grandpa, missing, grandma, more for
cousins plugged for meaning, scouts
thrown everywhere in seeds, bright corpuscles
dripping in the lodge – convention speaks
half-certainly of its impeccable credence:

She's a wonder with ideas, bloomed
like parsimony, gargantuan with labels
naming <u>hic</u> and <u>non</u>, estuary dribbles
outpatiently, robes and tissues gathered
in the glands, refusing food, refusing
water, ideas, conversings that will keep
the brain alive. A sleek longing like
panther nails clicks on her remembered
libido, as if someone drummed a
thumb there, her vincibility erupt.

———————

Sunset of circumstance, she's in the grease,
the aisles, squirming over the ground
of her competence, sing, of movement
we <u>can</u> 'take for granite' the call coming
over the waves, a river task given to us all,
children conglomerate looking backward
the eye musing on its livelihood.

———————

She's in the tile again – she looks
an aggregate glance, everyone is taken in.

'An orange face is a habit,' she declares,
looking over and over the shoulder of
the house, its eyes away from concentrated
wherewithal, children streaming, children
playing, the water rising closer each delay.
'That's a slow blood loses its armature,'
he wrote the electric daughter, and she
being habitual declined reply – beyond
the fencepost of the grave investment
we can be sure our indecision makes
no defense at all.

I'M NOT WAITING FOR ANYTHING

I will go unto my fatherless proclivities
and tickle them under their echoes
                                        I will finish

    the raimented air   languishing
                                                    encrusted

Such turpitude is exquisite, a myriad of vanishing lips
pushing back your mouth, your teeth, your tongue

    she can
          well imagine it

      the fumbling on your hands is
      mock gesture

          range pieces, where it never
        never was, believing scattered

   where it gathers
     the story is an infinitely small one, although

               it tells feelingly
barbed wire bristling in the echo

The Body Near as the Sea (a poem dance)

They enter smiling the trees
    removed and maladroit   collide

    Excuse the vaunting calipers:
    a manger of selective seas
    is riding up this way
        and reared-back
time a dreadful horse between

    A blessing on the heart-
    ed ground, spring as nothing t-
    o absorb the fingers
    needle-worked
        across   the dock

'She is constantly so reaching
    lights not yet, indeed not switched
at all her shadow stooped
    the semi-circle scene.'
        You sing

    Ex-usurpation through its tenets
stretch your hands: the little machines are
    fetch before you
        daring   black
    and white hearts   stet

Young and beautiful

The doll-face project is the one. articulately resonant.
A swimming pool swells with antipathy
for its prevenient material. as through a corner fabric
your eyes listening with Mirabel posture I can tell
quite luscious set round to approve.

Adventure rode the horse to shore. spoke it to admission
while warrants for the rest we cannot find.
You are listing ears full pearls that glisten tangy:
lust piled on emoluments, safe all round.

A fine plebiscite given the man sobbing by a fence,
a dove creaking without compromise.
Him I forestall and benedict. The swimming pool is
our vicissitudes, suited not then a body fit.
'Good enough for the traveling Egyptians, but
what about real music'.

Apraxia

I thought I had it – oh!, the scarified holds my limbs and it

I thought I had – the cure felt limpid scares and

here I thought soft voiced, the health-boy drunk to

waste of islands junket, boats tilted and one overboard

I thought I held, the paper – Care procures its vials

hold the sun the sheen palpates

You in bunches, a thread around your waists – slight meal

I thought I ate that, rolled and dightful tongue-melt up

you own man, you won suit gotten, you woven will it

thought we saw the same silt, the whole meal sat in adamant

fulfillment of said optioning, the land

I thought I had, elbow outward you sit throttled in the furrow

mazed, the somber man whith ides torn round

she woman own for lamp-lights, southern moon vents

that one held with etch in shoulders, with her garden garden

one soft round of lampshades, her bright offspring lapsed

I thought I had the sad eyes of the girl alight

she boat-set, rivers are the ops, feet the filled-in

Clemency of odds, I thought I had that

SOCIAL SCULPTURE

These appear the sun and boys and boys
their tan applications no hit but awful – these voices
so arrayed from ruination given to
a loftness or arising a blue
windmill lilting and not here
turning lot given a red way to say

'They feed themselves with suspicion'
'I think they are nominal and preventive'

No one dies for venture it's all 'durée'
she said with a dying voice the pieces of
your ideas taste stubby and sad about that
your brown hair falls swept back
your posture looks upright and lovely

They don't actually investigate
it's more like the serene face of the smiling
film-goddess harkening to partiality
she's gone and here the same
vitality due to form

Starter options finer than the face given to view
a domino effect – the body folds along its seams
and she is telling it increasingly rapids the bright water
falling across the fine green of her legs

she felt and the water gave a sense
we associate with men who leave dead
on the alternate wire that cuts through day
a point of view for the sake of energy procured.

a grace, hogwash, ratiocination, bodily projection,
a grey bonsai off an absent
flat small quantified.

ANACOLUTHON

that's that island there and I am not the day recedes
the man standing in a memory of the man standing
if I had a temple to relax in, it would be almond trees
those abeyed above our heads with mild bitterness
leaves tired having sprung in the spell
the news is over before it can be called –
it's a way of paying attention, that's the ticket
I have governed for someone's sake though has it been –
and lovely are the grasses, lovely the spell, the limbs cast upward
tellingly, his little hands climb the air, purposeful
(the youthful self he once was, lovely and externalized all nerves
and now embedded, imbued, re-tigered)
underneath the lemon tree all is forgiven
we suck until our voices ring like bells